Air Fryer Meat Cookbook

Easy & Delicious Best Air Fryer Meat Recipes ideas in 2021

Beck Wall

Copyright © 2021 by Beck Wall

This Book may not be reproduced, in part or in whole, without explicit permission and agreement by the Author by any means. This includes but is not limited to print, electronic media, scanning, photocopying, or file sharing.

The author has made every effort to ensure the accuracy of the information in the Book but assumes no responsibility should personal or commercial damage arise in the case of misinterpretation or misunderstanding. All suggestions, instructions, and guidelines expressed in the Book are meant for informational purposes only, and the reader assumes any and all risk when following said information.

Table of Contents

MILANESE CHOP	6
WORCESTERSHIRE BEEF MIX	7
GINGER BUTTERED STEAKS	8
PORK AND TOMATO SAUCE	9
FENNEL AND TOMATO PORK	10
ASPARAGUS AND BACON CASSEROLE	11
BEEF WITH AVOCADO AND CORN	12
CURRIED LAMB MEATBALLS	13
VEGETABLE CANE	14
PORK FILLET MIGNON	15
EGGPLANT BACON HUMMUS ROLLUPS	16
PORK CHOPS AND PESTO	17
LAMB AND ORANGE MIX	18
NEMOS BEEF WITH DRY PEPPER LACTOSE FREE	19
COCONUT LAMB	20
PORK SAUSAGES AND PEPPERS	21
CRISPY PORK MEDALLIONS	22
PORK WITH TOMATOES AND RED ONIONS	23
VEAL, SPECK, AND CHEESE PAUPIETTES	24
PORK CHOPS WITH CHICORY TREVISO	25
LEMON CHOPS	26
LAMB WITH PEANUTS	27
BACON VEGGIE CASSEROLE	28
INDIAN STYLE LAMB MEATBALLS	29
BRUSSELS AND ROASTED PORK CHOPS	30
MAPLE ROASTED PORK CHOPS AND VEGGIES	31
RED PEPPER MEATBALLS	32
ROAST PORK WITH VEGETABLES	33
SALTIMBOCCA ROMAN VEAL	34
LAMB CASSEROLE	35
LAMB AND MUSHROOMS MIX	36
MINTY LAMB CHOPS	37

CURRY BRUSSELS AND LAMB CHOPS	38
BRUSSELS, TOMATOES AND PORK CHOPS	39
JALAPENO LAMB CHOPS	40
PORK AND PARSNI WITH THAI, MARINATED WITH HONEY AND SOY	41
CURRY PORK CHOPS	42
SPINACH AND BACON CASSEROLE	43
LAMB WITH CARROTS AND APPLES MIX	44
PORK AND SHRIMP MIX	45
MUSHROOM AND BACON FRITTERS	46
VENETIAN LIVER	47
CEVAPI	48
GROUND BEEF AND CHORIZO MIX	49
SPINACH AND MAPLE BACON CASSEROLE	50
CHEESY BACON ROLLUPS	51
BEEF AND POTATO CURRY	52
SAUTÉED PORK WITH PEPPERS	53
CHEESY BACON FRITTERS	54
BEEF AND LEEKS	55
LEMON GARLIC LAMB CHOPS	56
MILANESE VEAL LEGS	57
CHIVES BEEF AND PORK STEW	58
BASIL BEEF	59
LAMB AND CAULIFLOWER MIX	60
AMATRICIANA	61
SWEET VEGGIES ROASTED PORK CHOPS	62
ZUCCHINI BACON ROLLUPS	63
EXTRA JUICY MEATBALLS	64
CAULIFLOWER AND BACON FRITTERS	65
SPICY MEATBALLS	66
BEEF WITH LENTILS AND KIDNEY BEANS	67
CHILI GROUND BEEF MIX	68
FRIED PORK	69
PERFECT GARLIC BUTTER STEAK	70

Dijon Roasted Pork Chops 71
Lamb and Peppers Mix 72
Coriander Pork Steaks 73
Eggplant Bacon Caprese Rollups 74
Veggies Roasted Pork Chops 75
Bacon and Cheese Casserole 76
Lamb Meatballs 77
Beef, Corn and Sweet Potatoes 78
Sautéed Meat with Potatoes 79
Lamb with Potatoes 80
Garlic and Lime Beef 81
Veal Blanquette With Peas 82
Broccoli and Bacon Fritters 83
Meatballs with Tomatoes and Peas 84
Beef Stroganoff 85
Baharat Lamb Meatballs 86
Lamb and Shallots Mix 87

Milanese Chop

Prep time: 10 – 20

Cook time: 15 – 30

Servings: 2

INGREDIENTS

- 2 veal chops
- 1 egg
- 70 g of breadcrumbs
- Salt to taste
- 1 tsp oil

INSTRUCTIONS

1. Beat the egg in a bowl and prepare the breadcrumbs on a flat plate.
2. Pass each chop in the egg and then in breadcrumbs. Press the meat firmly into the pie. Put in the refrigerator for at least half an hour.
3. Pour the oil into the basket. Place the two chops.
4. Set the air fryer to 1500 and cook the meat for 10 minutes and then turn the chop.
5. Cook for 5 minutes additional.
6. Serve the chops still hot, covering the bone with aluminum foil to facilitate tasting.

Worcestershire Beef Mix

Prep time: 10 minutes

Cook time: 30 minutes

Servings: 4

INGREDIENTS

- 2 pounds beef stew meat, cubed
- 1 red onion, chopped
- ½ teaspoon coriander, ground
- ½ cup canned tomatoes, crushed
- ½ cup beef stock
- 1 tablespoon Worcestershire sauce
- 1 tablespoon rosemary, chopped
- Salt and black pepper to the taste

INSTRUCTIONS

1. In a pan that fits your air fryer, combine the beef with the onion and the other ingredients, toss and cook at 400 degrees F for 30 minutes.
2. Divide everything between plates and serve.

Ginger Buttered Steaks

Prep time: 10 minutes

Cook time: 30 minutes

Servings: 4

INGREDIENTS

- 1 tablespoon ginger, grated
- 3 tablespoons butter, melted
- 2 pounds flank steaks
- 1 teaspoon mustard seeds, crushed
- 1 teaspoon sweet paprika
- Salt and black pepper to the taste
- 1 teaspoon rosemary, dried

INSTRUCTIONS

1. In your air fryer's basket, mix the steaks with the melted butter and the other ingredients, rub and cook at 390 degrees F for 15 minutes on each side.
2. Serve the steaks with a side salad.

Pork and Tomato Sauce

Prep time: 10 minutes

Cook time: 35 minutes

Servings: 4

INGREDIENTS

- 2 pounds pork stew meat, cubed
- 1 red onion, chopped
- ½ teaspoon chili powder
- ½ teaspoon coriander, ground
- 2 garlic cloves, minced
- 2 cups tomato sauce
- Salt and black pepper to the taste
- ½ bunch parsley, chopped

INSTRUCTIONS

1. In the air fryer's pan, mix the pork with the onion and the other ingredients and toss.
2. Introduce the pan in the fryer, cook at 380 degrees F for 35 minutes, divide between plates and serve.

Fennel and Tomato Pork

Prep time: 10 minutes

Cook time: 25 minutes

Servings: 4

INGREDIENTS

- 2 pounds pork chops
- 2 fennel bulbs, sliced
- 2 tomatoes, cubed
- 2 tablespoons olive oil
- ½ teaspoon chili powder
- ½ teaspoon coriander, ground
- Salt and black pepper to the taste
- 1 teaspoon fennel seeds, roasted
- 1 tablespoon chives, chopped

INSTRUCTIONS

1. In the air fryer's pan, mix the pork chops with the fennel and the other ingredients, toss and cook at 400 degrees F for 25 minutes.
2. Divide the mix between plates and serve.

Asparagus and Bacon Casserole

Prep time: 10 minutes

Cook time: 30 minutes

Servings: 12

INGREDIENTS

- 16 eggs
- ¼ cup whole milk
- 1 cup cooked, sliced bacon
- 1 pound chopped asparagus
- 1 cup cheddar cheese, grated
- ½ cup grated parmesan cheese
- ½ cup whole milk ricotta
- ¼ cup chopped white onion
- 1 tsp minced garlic
- 1 tsp sea salt
- ½ tsp dried thyme
- ½ tsp ground black pepper

INSTRUCTIONS

1. Preheat your air fryer to 350 degrees F and prepare a large baking dish with baking grease (make sure the pan will fit in your air fryer.
2. Whisk the eggs and milk in a large bowl.
3. Add the bacon and asparagus to the egg mix.
4. Add all the remaining ingredients, except the ricotta, and stir well.
5. Pour the egg and veggie mix into the prepared tray.
6. Dollop the ricotta around the pan, dispersing it evenly.
7. Bake in the air fryer for 30 minutes or until the eggs are completely set.

Beef with Avocado and Corn

Prep time: 10 minutes

Cook time: 25 minutes

Servings: 2

INGREDIENTS

- 1 pound beef stew meat, cubed
- 1 cup avocado, peeled, pitted and cubed
- 1 cup corn
- 2 tablespoons olive oil
- 2 tablespoons balsamic vinegar
- Salt and black pepper to the taste
- 1 tablespoon chives, chopped

INSTRUCTIONS

1. In a pan that fits your air fryer, mix the beef with the avocado, corn and the other ingredients, introduce the pan in the fryer and cook at 390 degrees F for 25 minutes.
2. Divide everything between plates and serve.

Curried Lamb Meatballs

Prep time: 10 minutes

Cook time: 25 minutes

Servings: 4

INGREDIENTS
- 1 pound ground lamb
- ¾ cup feta cheese
- ¼ cup fresh grated parmesan
- 1 tsp curry seasoning
- ¼ tsp ground black pepper
- ¼ tsp salt
- 1 Tbsp coconut flour

INSTRUCTIONS
1. Preheat your air fryer to 350 degrees F and line the air fryer tray with a piece of foil.
2. In a large mixing bowl, combine the lamb, cheeses, curry seasoning, pepper, salt and almond flour. Blend together well.
3. Roll the meat mixture into evenly sized balls and place on the prepared tray.
4. Bake for 25 minutes.
5. Serve the meatballs while hot!

Vegetable Cane

Prep time: 10-20 minutes

Cook time: more than 60 minutes

Servings: 4

INGREDIENTS

- 2 calf legs
- 4 carrots
- 4 medium potatoes
- 1 clove garlic
- 300ml Broth
- Leave to taste
- Pepper to taste

INSTRUCTIONS

1. Place the ears, garlic, and half of the broth in the greased basket.
2. Set the temperature to 180oC.
3. Cook the stems for 40 minutes, turning them in the middle of cooking.
4. Add the vegetables in pieces, salt, pepper, pour the rest of the broth and cook for another 50 minutes (time may vary depending on the size of the hocks).
5. Mix the vegetables and the ears 2 to 3 times during cooking.

Pork Fillet Mignon

Prep time: 5 minutes

Cook time: 12 minutes

Servings: 3

INGREDIENTS

- 6 medallions of 100g to 150g cut in a pork loin
- Olive oil
- Salt and pepper

INSTRUCTIONS

1. Cut six pork medallions the same size as the pork loin you own.
2. Salt and pepper to your liking.
3. Use a cooking tool to spray a very small amount of olive oil.
4. Place your pork medallions on the air fryer previously preheated at 1500C and cook for 12 minutes.
5. **NUTRITION:**
6. Calories 125
7. Fat 3.4g
8. Carbohydrates 0g
9. Sugars 0g
10. Protein 22g
11. Cholesterol 62mg

Eggplant Bacon Hummus Rollups

Prep time: 5 minutes

Cook time: 8 minutes

Servings: 8

INGREDIENTS

- 1 eggplant, sliced thinly lengthwise
- ¼ cup keto hummus
- 4 oz mozzarella cheese, sliced
- 8 strips bacon
- 2 Tbsp chopped fresh basil
- 2 Tbsp olive oil

INSTRUCTIONS

1. Preheat your air fryer to 400 degrees F and prepare a large baking dish with foil.
2. Lay the eggplant slices out on a clean work surface.
3. Spread hummus on each eggplant slice.
4. Place a piece of cheese and a little basil on each eggplant slice and then roll up to enclose the filling.
5. Wrap a strip of bacon around the outside of each rollup.
6. Secure using a toothpick and then place the eggplant rolls on the prepared foil lined baking dish.
7. Drizzle with the olive oil and place in the air fryer to cook for 8 minutes. The eggplant should be lightly brown and the cheese melted. Serve warm.

Pork Chops and Pesto

Prep time: 10 minutes

Cook time: 25 minutes

Servings: 4

INGREDIENTS

- 2 pounds pork chops
- 2 tablespoons basil pesto
- 1 cup beef stock
- Salt and black pepper to the taste
- ½ teaspoon garam masala
- ½ teaspoon turmeric powder

INSTRUCTIONS

1. In a pan that fits your air fryer, mix the pork chops with the pesto and the other ingredients, toss, introduce the pan the fryer and cook at 400 degrees F for 25 minutes.
2. Divide everything between plates and serve.

Lamb and Orange Mix

Prep time: 10 minutes

Cook time: 25 minutes

Servings: 4

INGREDIENTS

- 2 pounds lamb chops
- Juice of 1 orange
- 1 orange, peeled and cut into segments
- 2 tablespoons olive oil
- A pinch of salt and black pepper
- ½ tablespoon lemon peel, grated
- 1 tablespoon oregano, chopped
- ½ teaspoon rosemary, dried

INSTRUCTIONS

1. In the air fryer's pan, mix the lamb chops with the orange juice and the other ingredients, toss, cook at 400 degrees F for 25 minutes, divide between plates and serve.

Nemos Beef with Dry Pepper Lactose Free

Prep time: 30 minutes

Cook time: 20-25 minutes

Servings: 5

INGREDIENTS

- 250g of minced meat
- 1 handful of rice noodles
- 25 rice leaves
- 1 small onion
- 1 clove garlic
- 1 cube of chicken broth
- Roasted Sesame Oil
- 2 tsp dried pepper
- 1 tbsp soy sauce
- 1 tsp ground ginger

INSTRUCTIONS

1. Finely chop the onion and garlic and mix with the minced meat. Add half of the dried pepper, being careful to crush it beforehand. Add the ginger powder and soy sauce. Brown the preparation in roasted sesame oil, making sure you only have small pieces of minced meat.
2. Bring a pan of boiling water to which you will add chicken broth. Dip the rice noodles in it for only 3 minutes.
3. Add them to the ground beef preparation and then add the rest of the dried pepper.
4. Lightly moisten the rice leaves, place the filling in the middle and close them to create a perfect nem.
5. Place the spring rolls in the air fryer without oil previously heated at 150oC and cook for 10 to 15 minutes, according to taste.

Coconut Lamb

Prep time: 10 minutes

Cook time: 25 minutes

Servings: 4

INGREDIENTS

- 1 pound lamb chops
- 1 cup coconut cream
- 1 teaspoon curry powder
- 2 tablespoons butter, melted
- 1 tablespoon rosemary, chopped
- ½ teaspoon garam masala
- Juice of 1 lime
- Salt and black pepper to the taste

INSTRUCTIONS

1. In the air fryer's pan, mix the lamb chops with the cream and the other ingredients, toss well, introduce the pan in the fryer and cook at 400 degrees F for 25 minutes.
2. Divide the mix between plates and serve.

Pork Sausages and Peppers

Prep time: 10 minutes

Cook time: 20 minutes

Servings: 4

INGREDIENTS

- 1 pound pork sausage links, roughly sliced
- 1 cup roasted bell peppers, cut into strips
- 1 green bell pepper, cut into strips
- Juice of 1 lime
- 1 teaspoon sweet paprika
- 1 teaspoon chili powder
- 1 tablespoon olive oil
- Salt and black pepper to the taste
- 2 garlic cloves, minced

INSTRUCTIONS

1. In a pan that fits your air fryer, mix the sausage with the peppers and the other ingredients, introduce the pan in the fryer and cook at 360 degrees F for 20 minutes.
2. Divide between plates and serve hot.

Crispy Pork Medallions

Prep time: 20 minutes

Cook time: 5 minutes

Servings: 2

INGREDIENTS

- 1 pork loin, 330 g, cut into 6 or 7 slices of 4 cm
- 1 tsp Dijon mustard
- 1 tsp oil
- Salt, pepper and paprika
- Asian marinade
- 1 tsp salt reduced tamari sauce
- 1 tsp olive oil
- 1 clementine juice
- 1 pinch cayenne pepper
- 2 cloves garlic, pressed
- Crunchy coating
- 1/3 cup breadcrumbs
- ½ orange zest
- 2g freshly grated Parmesan cheese

INSTRUCTIONS

1. Prepare the marinade first. In a bowl, combine all the ingredients. Lightly salt the medallions, pepper, and sprinkle with paprika. Place these in the marinade and turn them several times to impregnate them completely. Cover with plastic wrap and marinate for 1 hour at room temperature.
2. Prepare the coating by combining the breadcrumbs, the orange zest, and the Parmesan cheese in a deep dish.
3. When the maceration time has elapsed, remove the marinade medallions, and dry them on absorbent paper. Spread with mustard, then move on to the crunchy layer. Brush lightly with oil.
4. Heat the air fryer to 350°F. Place the medallions in the fryer basket. Cook 5 minutes, stir, and then return to the fryer for another minute. Serve immediately.

Pork with Tomatoes and Red Onions

Prep time: 10 minutes

Cook time: 20 minutes

Servings: 4

INGREDIENTS

- 1 pound pork tenderloin, cubed
- 2 tomatoes, cubed
- 2 red onions, sliced
- 2 tablespoons olive oil
- ½ teaspoon hot chili powder
- Salt and black pepper to the taste
- 1 tablespoon parsley, chopped

INSTRUCTIONS

1. In your air fryer's pan, mix the pork with the tomatoes and the other ingredients, toss and cook at 380 degrees F for 20 minutes.
2. Divide everything between plates and serve.

VEAL, SPECK, AND CHEESE PAUPIETTES

Prep time: 10-20 minutes

Cook time: 15-30 minutes

Servings: 6

INGREDIENTS
- 12 slices of veal
- 6 speck slices
- 12 slices of provola
- Salt to taste
- Pepper to taste

INSTRUCTIONS
1. Place half a slice of stain and one of provola on each slice of veal; Roll each slice and close them with toothpicks.
2. Pour the oil and place the paupiettes in the basket, season with salt and pepper.
3. Set the air fryer to 180oC.
4. Cook the paupiettes for 15 minutes, turning them around after about 8 to 9 minutes.

Pork Chops with Chicory Treviso

Prep time: 10-20

Cook time: 0-15

Servings: 2

INGREDIENTS
- 4 pork chops
- 40g butter
- Flour to taste
- 1 chicory stalk
- Salt to taste

INSTRUCTIONS
1. Cut the chicory into small pieces. Place the butter and chicory in pieces on the basket of the air fryer previously preheated at 180oC and brown for 2 min.
2. Add the previously floured and salted pork slices (directly over the chicory), simmer for 6 minutes turning them over after 3 minutes.
3. Remove the slices and place them on a serving plate, covering them with the rest of the red chicory juice collected at the bottom of the basket.

Lemon Chops

Prep time: 0-10

Cook time: 0-15

Servings: 2

INGREDIENTS

- 4 slices of pork
- 40g butter
- Flour to taste
- 1 lemon juice
- Salt to taste

INSTRUCTIONS

1. Preheat the air fryer at 180oC for 5 minutes.
2. Flour the pork slices. Place the butter in the basket and brown for 2 minutes.
3. Add the previously floured and salted pork slices, simmer for 3 another minutes. Turn them on themselves.
4. Add the lemon juice and simmer for 3another minutes.
5. Remove the slices and add a pinch of butter to the tank to thicken the juice. Mix the juice with a wooden spoon and pour the scallops over it.
6. Serve decorating the dish with lemon julienne.

Lamb with Peanuts

Prep time: 10 minutes

Cook time: 25 minutes

Servings: 4

INGREDIENTS

- 2 pounds lamb stew meat, cubed
- 1 cup peanuts, chopped
- 1 cup spring onions, chopped
- 2 tablespoons olive oil
- 1 teaspoon cumin, ground
- 2 garlic cloves, minced
- ½ cup coconut milk
- Salt and black pepper to the taste

INSTRUCTIONS

1. In a pan that fits your air fryer, mix the lamb with the peanuts and the other ingredients, toss, introduce the pan in the fryer and cook at 400 degrees F for 25 minutes.
2. Divide into bowls and serve.

BACON VEGGIE CASSEROLE

Prep time: 10 minutes
Cook time: 30 minutes
Servings: 12

INGREDIENTS

- 16 eggs
- ¼ cup whole milk
- 1 cup cooked, sliced bacon
- 10 oz frozen, chopped spinach, thawed, drained
- 2 cups chopped asparagus
- ½ cup sundried tomatoes, chopped
- 1 cup cheddar cheese, grated
- ½ cup grated parmesan cheese
- ½ cup whole milk ricotta
- ¼ cup chopped white onion
- 1 tsp minced garlic
- 1 tsp sea salt
- ½ tsp dried thyme
- ½ tsp ground black pepper

INSTRUCTIONS

1. Preheat your air fryer to 350 degrees F and prepare a large baking dish with baking grease (make sure the pan will fit in your air fryer.
2. Whisk the eggs and milk in a large bowl.
3. Add the bacon, asparagus, tomatoes and spinach to the egg mix.
4. Add all the remaining ingredients, except the ricotta, and stir well.
5. Pour the egg and veggie mix into the prepared tray.
6. Dollop the ricotta around the pan, dispersing it evenly.
7. Bake in the air fryer for 30 minutes or until the eggs are completely set.

Indian Style Lamb Meatballs

Prep time: 10 minutes

Cook time: 25 minutes

Servings: 4

INGREDIENTS

- 1 pound ground lamb
- ¾ cup halloumi cheese, shredded
- ¼ cup fresh grated parmesan
- 1 tsp cumin
- ½ tsp turmeric
- ¼ tsp ground black pepper
- ¼ tsp salt
- 1 Tbsp almond flour

INSTRUCTIONS

1. Preheat your air fryer to 350 degrees F and line the air fryer tray with a piece of foil.
2. In a large mixing bowl, combine the lamb, cheeses, cumin, turmeric, pepper, salt and almond flour. Blend together well.
3. Roll the meat mixture into evenly sized balls and place on the prepared tray.
4. Bake for 25 minutes.
5. Serve the meatballs while hot!

Brussels and Roasted Pork Chops

Prep time: 20 minutes

Cook time: 30 minutes

Servings: 6

INGREDIENTS

- 2 pounds Pork Chops, bone-in
- ½ tsp salt
- ½ tsp ground black pepper
- 3 carrots, chopped
- 2 celery stalks, chopped
- ½ pound Brussels Sprouts, sliced in half
- 1 Tbsp minced garlic
- 3 Tbsp butter, melted
- ½ cup white onion, chopped
- 1 tsp dried thyme
- ½ tsp dried rosemary

INSTRUCTIONS

1. Preheat your air fryer to 425 degrees F and prepare your air fryer tray with a piece of foil.
2. Rub the pork chops with the salt and pepper, wrap and let sit overnight to season.
3. Place the onion, carrot, celery, Brussels and garlic on the prepared foil lined tray.
4. Place the pork chops on top of the veggies.
5. Brush the pork chops with the melted butter and sprinkle with the thyme and rosemary.
6. Bake in the air fryer for 30 minutes or until the chicken thighs are browned and the veggies are beginning to brown as well.
7. Serve hot.

Maple Roasted Pork Chops and Veggies

Prep time: 20 minutes

Cook time: 30 minutes

Servings: 6

INGREDIENTS

- 2 pounds Pork Chops, bone-in
- ½ tsp salt
- ½ tsp ground black pepper
- 1 tsp maple extract
- 3 carrots, chopped
- 2 celery stalks, chopped
- 1 Tbsp minced garlic
- 3 Tbsp butter, melted
- ½ cup white onion, chopped
- 1 tsp dried thyme
- ½ tsp dried rosemary

INSTRUCTIONS

1. Preheat your air fryer to 425 degrees F and prepare your air fryer tray with a piece of foil.
2. Rub the pork chops with the salt, pepper, and maple extract and wrap and let sit overnight to season.
3. Place the onion, carrot, celery and garlic on the prepared foil lined tray.
4. Place the pork chops on top of the veggies.
5. Brush the pork chops with the melted butter and sprinkle with the thyme and rosemary.
6. Bake in the air fryer for 30 minutes or until the chicken thighs are browned and the veggies are beginning to brown as well.
7. Serve hot.

Red Pepper Meatballs

Prep time: 10 minutes

Cook time: 25 minutes

Servings: 4

INGREDIENTS

- 1 pound ground beef
- ¾ cup mozzarella cheese, shredded
- ½ cup diced red peppers
- ¼ cup fresh grated parmesan
- 1 tsp Italian seasoning
- ¼ tsp ground black pepper
- ¼ tsp salt
- 1 Tbsp almond flour

INSTRUCTIONS

1. Preheat your air fryer to 350 degrees F and line the air fryer tray with a piece of foil.
2. In a large mixing bowl, combine the beef, cheeses, red peppers, Italian seasoning, pepper, salt and almond flour. Blend together well.
3. Roll the meat mixture into evenly sized balls and place on the prepared tray.
4. Bake for 25 minutes.
5. Serve the meatballs while hot!

Roast Pork with Vegetables

Prep time: 10-20 minutes

Cook time: more than 60 minutes

Servings: 8

INGREDIENTS
- 1 kg of pork loin
- 4 carrots
- 3 potatoes
- 1 onion
- 1 clove garlic
- 250 ml broth
- Salt and pepper to taste

INSTRUCTIONS
1. Place the tenderloin in the center of the tank, as well as the vegetables in small pieces, salt, pepper and pour a little broth.
2. Set the temperature to 160ºC. Simmer for 1 hour and 30 minutes. Mix the vegetables occasionally and turn the loin halfway through cooking. Add some broth as necessary to keep the meat tender.

Saltimbocca Roman Veal

Prep time: 10 – 20 minutes

Cook time: 0 – 15 minutes

Servings: 4

INGREDIENTS

- 70-80 g See
- 16 slices of raw ham
- 16 sage leaves
- 20 g butter
- Salt to taste
- Pepper to taste
- Address:
- Place the meat slices on a sheet of parchment paper. Arrange the ham slices on the meat, put the washed sage leaf, roll, and close with a toothpick.
- Place the butter in the basket at 1500C. Melt the butter for 2 min.
- Add the meat and simmer for 6 minutes.

Lamb Casserole

Prep time: 10 minutes
Cook time: 35 minutes
Servings: 4

INGREDIENTS

- 2 pounds lamb stew meat, ground and browned
- 1 cup mozzarella cheese, shredded
- 1 cup cherry tomatoes, halved
- 1 cup zucchini, cubed
- 1 yellow onion, chopped
- ½ cup heavy cream
- Cooking spray
- Salt and black pepper to the taste

INSTRUCTIONS

1. Grease a baking dish that fits your air fryer with the cooking spray and mix the lamb with the tomatoes and the other ingredients except the cheese inside.
2. Sprinkle the cheese on top, introduce the dish in the air fryer and cook at 380 degrees F for 35 minutes.
3. Divide between plates and serve.

Lamb and Mushrooms Mix

Prep time: 10 minutes
Cook time: 35 minutes
Servings: 4

INGREDIENTS

- 2 pounds lamb chops
- 1 cup white mushrooms, halved
- 1 red onion, chopped
- 1 cup heavy cream
- 2 tablespoons butter, melted
- 1 teaspoon chili powder
- Salt and black pepper to the taste
- 1 tablespoon cilantro, chopped

INSTRUCTIONS

1. In the air fryer's pan, mix the lamb chops with the mushrooms and the other ingredients, toss, introduce the pan in the fryer and cook at 380 degrees F for 35 minutes.
2. Divide everything between plates and serve.

Minty Lamb Chops

Prep time: 20 minutes

Cook time: 30 minutes

Servings: 4

INGREDIENTS

1. 3 Tbsp olive oil
2. 3 Tbsp lemon juice
3. 1 Tbsp fresh chopped mint
4. 1 pound lamb chops
5. ½ tsp sea salt
6. ¼ tsp ground black pepper
7. 1 zucchini, sliced thinly
8. 3 cups baby spinach

INSTRUCTIONS

1. Preheat your air fryer to 400 degrees F and prepare your air fryer tray with a piece of foil.
2. In a large bowl, whisk together 2 Tbsp of the olive oil, lemon juice, and mint.
3. Add the lamb chops to the bowl and toss to coat. Cover the bowl and place in the fridge for two hours.
4. Add the remaining tablespoon of olive oil to a saute pan and heat over high. Sear the marinated lamb chops on each side for 3 minutes, just to brown.
5. Move the browned pork lamb to the prepared, foil lined tray and pour the remaining marinade from the bowl over the chops.
6. Add the zucchini and baby spinach, placing them over and around the lamb chops.
7. Place the tray in the preheated air fryer for 20 minutes. Serve hot.

Curry Brussels and Lamb Chops

Prep time: 20 minutes

Cook time: 30 minutes

Servings: 4

INGREDIENTS
- 3 Tbsp olive oil
- 3 Tbsp lemon juice
- 3 Tbsp minced garlic
- 1 pound lamb chops
- ½ tsp sea salt
- 1 tsp curry powder
- 1 pound sliced Brussels sprouts
- 1 lemon, sliced thinly

INSTRUCTIONS
1. Preheat your air fryer to 400 degrees F and prepare your air fryer tray with a piece of foil.
2. In a large bowl, whisk together 2 Tbsp of the olive oil, curry powder, lemon juice, and garlic.
3. Add the lamb chops to the bowl and toss to coat. Cover the bowl and place in the fridge for two hours.
4. Add the remaining tablespoon of olive oil to a saute pan and heat over high. Sear the marinated lamb chops on each side for 3 minutes, just to brown.
5. Move the browned pork lamb to the prepared, foil lined tray and pour the remaining marinade from the bowl over the chops.
6. Add the Brussels and lemon slices, layering them over and around the lamb chops.
7. Place the tray in the preheated air fryer for 20 minutes. Serve hot.

Brussels, Tomatoes and Pork Chops

Prep time: 20 minutes

Cook time: 30 minutes

Servings: 4

INGREDIENTS

- 3 Tbsp olive oil
- 3 Tbsp lemon juice
- 3 Tbsp minced garlic
- 1 tsp oregano, dried
- 1 pound pork chops
- ½ tsp sea salt
- ¼ tsp ground black pepper
- 1 pound Brussel sprouts sliced in half
- ¼ cup chopped sundried tomatoes
- 1 lemon, sliced thinly

INSTRUCTIONS

1. Preheat your air fryer to 400 degrees F and prepare your air fryer tray with a piece of foil.
2. In a large bowl, whisk together 2 Tbsp of the olive oil, lemon juice, dried oregano and garlic.
3. Add the pork chops to the bowl and toss to coat. Cover the bowl and place in the fridge for two hours.
4. Add the remaining tablespoon of olive oil to a saute pan and heat over high. Sear the marinated pork chops on each side for 3 minutes, just to brown.
5. Move the browned pork chops to the prepared, foil lined tray and pour the remaining marinade from the bowl over the chops.
6. Add the Brussels, sundried tomatoes and lemon slices, layering them over and around the pork chops.
7. Place the tray in the preheated air fryer for 20 minutes. Serve hot.

Jalapeno Lamb Chops

Prep time: 10 minutes

Cook time: 35 minutes

Servings: 4

INGREDIENTS

- 2 pounds lamb chops
- 2 jalapenos, chopped
- Salt and black pepper to the taste
- ½ cup coconut cream
- 2 garlic cloves, chopped
- 2 tablespoons butter, melted
- 3 tablespoons chili powder

INSTRUCTIONS

1. In the air fryer's pan, mix the lamb chops with the jalapenos and the other ingredients, introduce the pan in the air fryer and cook at 380 degrees F for 35 minutes.
2. Divide everything between plates and serve.

PORK AND PARSNI WITH THAI, MARINATED WITH HONEY AND SOY

Prep time: 20 minutes

Cook time: 30 minutes

Servings: 2

INGREDIENTS
- 2 pork ribs to choose from the tenderloin
- 1 large parsnip
- 1 coriander leaf
- 1 sprig fresh chopped parsley
- Salt
- For the marinade:
- 2 tbsp olive oil
- 2 tbsp soy sauce
- The juice of half a lemon
- 1 tbsp of honey, preferably flavored with orange blossom
- 1 tsp of specific spices for wok preparation
- 1 tsp of Asian spice mix
- Coriander powder

INSTRUCTIONS
1. Prepare the marinade by mixing all the ingredients in a large bowl. Mix to obtain a very homogeneous mixture.
2. Dip the pork chunks in the marinade, turning them over to make sure it covers the meat ribs perfectly. Prepare the parsnip by peeling and washing it, and then cut it into small dice.
3. Use a large plate to place the pieces of pork and parsnips covered with marinade. Pour the parsnips into the bowl and mix. Let stand for at least 1 hour before cooking.
4. Set the air fryer at 160oC without oil for 30 minutes and cook the parsnips.
5. At the end of the 10 minutes of cooking, add the pieces of pork or proceed to a traditional baking in the oven with 10 minutes on each side being careful to keep the cooking juices.

Curry Pork Chops

Prep time: 10 minutes

Cook time: 25 minutes

Servings: 4

INGREDIENTS

- 2 tablespoons red curry paste
- 2 tablespoons olive oil
- 1 teaspoon chili powder
- 1 teaspoon curry powder
- 2 pounds pork chops
- 2 tablespoons chives, chopped
- Salt and black pepper to the taste

INSTRUCTIONS

1. In your air fryer's basket, combine the pork chops with the curry paste and the other ingredients, rub and cook at 400 degrees F for 25 minutes.
2. Divide the mix between plates and serve with a side salad.

SPINACH AND BACON CASSEROLE

Prep time: 10 minutes

Cook time: 30 minutes

Servings: 12

INGREDIENTS

- 16 eggs
- ¼ cup whole milk
- 1 cup cooked, sliced bacon
- 10 oz frozen, chopped spinach, thawed, drained
- 1 cup cheddar cheese, grated
- ½ cup grated parmesan cheese
- ½ cup whole milk ricotta
- ¼ cup chopped white onion
- 1 tsp minced garlic
- 1 tsp sea salt
- ½ tsp dried thyme
- ½ tsp ground black pepper

INSTRUCTIONS

1. Preheat your air fryer to 350 degrees F and prepare a large baking dish with baking grease (make sure the pan will fit in your air fryer.
2. Whisk the eggs and milk in a large bowl.
3. Add the bacon and spinach to the egg mix.
4. Add all the remaining ingredients, except the ricotta, and stir well.
5. Pour the egg and veggie mix into the prepared tray.
6. Dollop the ricotta around the pan, dispersing it evenly.
7. Bake in the air fryer for 30 minutes or until the eggs are completely set.

Lamb with Carrots and Apples Mix

Prep time: 10 minutes

Cook time: 30 minutes

Servings: 4

INGREDIENTS

- 2 pounds lamb stew meat, cubed
- 1 cup carrots, peeled and sliced
- 1 cup apples, cored and cubed
- 2 tablespoons olive oil
- ½ cup beef stock
- Salt and black pepper to the taste
- ½ teaspoon smoked paprika

INSTRUCTIONS

1. In the air fryer's pan, mix the lamb with the carrots and the other ingredients, toss, transfer the pan to your air fryer and cook at 380 degrees F for 30 minutes.
2. Divide the mix into bowls and serve.

Pork and Shrimp Mix

Prep time: 10 minutes

Cook time: 30 minutes

Servings: 4

INGREDIENTS

- 2 pounds pork stew meat, cubed
- ½ pound shrimp, peeled and deveined
- Salt and black pepper to the taste
- 1 tablespoons olive oil
- ½ teaspoon chili powder
- ½ teaspoon sweet paprika
- ½ cup beef stock
- 2 tablespoons oregano, chopped

INSTRUCTIONS

1. In the air fryer's pan, mix the pork with the chili powder and the other ingredients except the shrimp, toss and cook at 370 degrees F for 20 minutes.
2. Add the shrimp, cook the mix for 10 minutes more, divide into bowls and serve.

Mushroom and Bacon Fritters

Prep time: 10 minutes

Cook time: 30 minutes

Servings: 4

INGREDIENTS

- ¾ cup almond flour
- 7 Tbsp ground flaxseeds
- 1 ½ cup chopped mushrooms, fresh
- ½ cup cooked, crumbled bacon
- 4 ounces grated mozzarella cheese
- 2 eggs
- 2 tsp baking powder
- 1 tsp salt
- ¼ tsp ground black pepper
- 1 Tbsp olive oil

INSTRUCTIONS

1. Preheat your air fryer to 400 degrees F and prepare a large baking dish with foil.
2. Place the mushrooms in a food processor along with the mozzarella, bacon, almond flour, 4 tablespoons of the flaxseeds and baking powder. Pulse until the mixture reaches a crumbly texture.
3. Add the eggs, salt and pepper and pulse until a dough forms.
4. Scoop the mix into bite sized balls, rolling them between your hands.
5. Roll the balls in the remaining flaxseeds and place on the prepared baking tray.
6. Drizzle with the olive oil and roll the balls around on the tray so the olive oil is coating the outside.
7. Place in the preheated air fryer and bake for 10 minutes or until nicely golden brown. Enjoy hot.

Venetian Liver

Prep time: 10-20

Cook time: 15-30

Servings: 6

INGREDIENTS

- 500g veal liver
- 2 white onions
- 100g of water
- 2 tbsp vinegar
- Salt and pepper to taste

INSTRUCTIONS

1. Chop the onion and put it inside the pan with the water. Set the air fryer to 180oC and cook for 20 minutes.
2. Add the liver cut into small pieces and vinegar, close the lid, and cook for an additional 10 minutes.
3. Add salt and pepper.

CEVAPI

Prep time: more than 30

Cook time: 15 – 30

Servings: 4

INGREDIENTS

- 150g of onion
- 350g ground beef
- 150g minced pork
- Leave at discretion
- Pepper at discretion
- Red paprika at discretion

INSTRUCTIONS

1. Mix all the ingredients in a bowl (the onion must be finely chopped) and knead well; form rolls 4 to 5 cm long and let stand in the refrigerator for at least 1 hour.
2. Place the cevapi in the basket of the air fryer. Set the temperature to 150oC.
3. Cook the cevapis (8 at a time) for about 13 to 15 minutes, turning them in the middle of cooking.

Ground Beef and Chorizo Mix

Prep time: 10 minutes

Cook time: 20 minutes

Servings: 4

INGREDIENTS

- 1 pound beef stew meat, ground and browned
- 1 cup chorizo, chopped
- 1 red onion, chopped
- 1 red bell pepper, cut into strips
- 1 cup cherry tomatoes, halved
- 1 tablespoon olive oil
- Salt and black pepper to the taste
- 1 tablespoon thyme, chopped
- ½ cup beef stock

INSTRUCTIONS

1. In the air fryer's pan, mix the beef with the chorizo and the other ingredients and toss.
2. Introduce the pan in the fryer and cook at 390 degrees F for 20 minutes.
3. Divide the mix between and serve.

Spinach and Maple Bacon Casserole

Prep time: 10 minutes

Cook time: 30 minutes

Servings: 12

INGREDIENTS

- 16 eggs
- ¼ cup whole milk
- 1 cup cooked, sliced maple seasoned bacon
- 10 oz frozen, chopped spinach, thawed, drained
- 1 cup cheddar cheese, grated
- ½ cup grated parmesan cheese
- ½ cup whole milk ricotta
- ¼ cup chopped white onion
- 1 tsp minced garlic
- 1 tsp sea salt
- ½ tsp dried thyme
- ½ tsp ground black pepper

INSTRUCTIONS

1. Preheat your air fryer to 350 degrees F and prepare a large baking dish with baking grease (make sure the pan will fit in your air fryer.
2. Whisk the eggs and milk in a large bowl.
3. Add the bacon and spinach to the egg mix.
4. Add all the remaining ingredients, except the ricotta, and stir well.
5. Pour the egg and veggie mix into the prepared tray.
6. Dollop the ricotta around the pan, dispersing it evenly.
7. Bake in the air fryer for 30 minutes or until the eggs are completely set.

Cheesy Bacon Rollups

Prep time: 5 minutes

Cook time: 8 minutes

Servings: 8

INGREDIENTS

- 1 eggplant, sliced thinly lengthwise
- 4 oz mozzarella cheese, sliced
- ½ cup grated parmesan
- 8 strips bacon
- 2 Tbsp chopped fresh basil
- 2 Tbsp olive oil

INSTRUCTIONS

1. Preheat your air fryer to 400 degrees F and prepare a large baking dish with foil.
2. Lay the eggplant slices out on a clean work surface.
3. Place mozzarella, parmesan and a little basil on each eggplant slice and then roll up to enclose the filling.
4. Wrap a strip of bacon around the outside of each rollup.
5. Secure using a toothpick and then place the eggplant rolls on the prepared foil lined baking dish.
6. Drizzle with the olive oil and place in the air fryer to cook for 8 minutes. The eggplant should be lightly brown and the cheese melted. Serve warm.

BEEF AND POTATO CURRY

Prep time: 10 minutes

Cook time: 35 minutes

Servings: 4

INGREDIENTS
- 2 pounds beef meat, cubed
- 2 tablespoons butter, melted
- 1 cup heavy cream
- ½ pound gold potatoes, peeled and cubed
- 1 tablespoon curry powder
- 1 yellow onion, chopped
- ½ teaspoon turmeric powder
- Salt and black pepper to the taste

INSTRUCTIONS
1. In the air fryer's pan, mix the beef with the melted butter and the other ingredients, toss, transfer the pan to your air fryer and cook at 380 degrees F for 35 minutes.
2. Divide everything into bowls and serve.

Sautéed Pork with Peppers

Prep time: 10 – 20 minutes

Cook time: 15 – 30 minutes

Servings: 6

INGREDIENTS
- 600 g pieces of pork taken from the loin or shoulder
- 200 g of peppers
- 1 shallot
- Salt to taste
- Pepper to taste

INSTRUCTIONS :
1. Preheat the air fryer at 150oC for 5 minutes. Spray the basket.
2. Chop the shallot and cut the peppers into strips Place the shallot and oil in the basket then brown for 2 minutes.
3. Add the peppers and simmer for another 8 minutes.
4. Finally pour the pieces of pork, salt, pepper, and simmer for another 10 minutes.

Cheesy Bacon Fritters

Prep time: 10 minutes

Cook time: 30 minutes

Servings: 4

INGREDIENTS

- ¾ cup almond flour
- 7 Tbsp ground flaxseeds
- 1 cup cooked, crumbled bacon
- 4 ounces grated mozzarella cheese
- ½ cup grated parmesan
- 2 eggs
- 2 tsp baking powder
- 1 tsp salt
- ¼ tsp ground black pepper
- 1 Tbsp olive oil

INSTRUCTIONS

1. Preheat your air fryer to 400 degrees F and prepare a large baking dish with foil.
2. Place the mozzarella, parmesan, bacon, almond flour, 4 tablespoons of the flaxseeds and baking powder. Pulse until the mixture reaches a crumbly texture.
3. Add the eggs, salt and pepper and pulse until a dough forms.
4. Scoop the mix into bite sized balls, rolling them between your hands.
5. Roll the balls in the remaining flaxseeds and place on the prepared baking tray.
6. Drizzle with the olive oil and roll the balls around on the tray so the olive oil is coating the outside.
7. Place in the preheated air fryer and bake for 10 minutes or until nicely golden brown. Enjoy hot.

BEEF AND LEEKS

Prep time: 10 minutes

Cook time: 25 minutes

Servings: 4

INGREDIENTS

- 1 pound beef stew meat, roughly cubed
- 2 leeks, sliced
- 1 cup mild salsa
- 1 tablespoon olive oil
- Salt and black pepper to the taste
- ½ teaspoon coriander, ground
- ½ teaspoon rosemary, dried
- 1 tablespoon chives, chopped

INSTRUCTIONS

1. In a pan that fits your air fryer, mix the beef with the leeks and the other ingredients, toss, introduce the pan in the fryer and cook at 380 degrees F for 25 minutes.
2. Divide into bowls and serve.

Lemon Garlic Lamb Chops

Prep time: 20 minutes

Cook time: 30 minutes

Servings: 4

INGREDIENTS

- 3 Tbsp olive oil
- 3 Tbsp lemon juice
- 3 Tbsp minced garlic
- 1 pound lamb chops
- ½ tsp sea salt
- ¼ tsp ground black pepper
- ½ pound asparagus
- 1 zucchini, sliced thinly
- 1 lemon, sliced thinly

INSTRUCTIONS

1. Preheat your air fryer to 400 degrees F and prepare your air fryer tray with a piece of foil.
2. In a large bowl, whisk together 2 Tbsp of the olive oil, lemon juice, and garlic.
3. Add the lamb chops to the bowl and toss to coat. Cover the bowl and place in the fridge for two hours.
4. Add the remaining tablespoon of olive oil to a saute pan and heat over high. Sear the marinated lamb chops on each side for 3 minutes, just to brown.
5. Move the browned pork lamb to the prepared, foil lined tray and pour the remaining marinade from the bowl over the chops.
6. Add the asparagus, zucchini and lemon slices, layering them over and around the lamb chops.
7. Place the tray in the preheated air fryer for 20 minutes. Serve hot.

Milanese Veal Legs

Prep time: 10-20 minutes

Cook time: more than 60 minutes

Servings: 4

INGREDIENTS

- 1kg beef leg
- 1 onion
- 1 glass of white wine
- 150g hot broth
- Taste Flour
- Salt, pepper to taste
- 1 bunch of parsley
- ½ grated lemon
- 1 clove garlic

INSTRUCTIONS

1. Place the chopped onion in the basket. Brown for 4 minutes at 1500C.
2. Add the lightly floured ears the white wine, season with salt and pepper and simmer for 6 minutes.
3. Turn the spikes, add the broth, and cook for another 50 minutes turning the meat 1-2 times.
4. At this point, add the chopped parsley, a grated peel of half a lemon and a clove of garlic and continue cooking for the remaining 10 minutes.
5. Serve hot with the juice that has formed in the cooking vessel.

Chives Beef and Pork Stew

Prep time: 10 minutes

Cook time: 35 minutes

Servings: 4

INGREDIENTS

- 2 tablespoons olive oil
- 1 pound beef stew meat, cubed
- 1 pound pork stew meat, cubed
- 1 cup canned tomatoes, crushed
- 1 carrot, sliced
- 1 zucchini, cubed
- 2 tablespoons chives, minced
- 3 garlic cloves, minced
- Salt and black pepper to the taste
- ½ cup beef stock

INSTRUCTIONS

1. In the air fryer's pan, mix the beef with the pork and the other ingredients, toss and cook at 390 degrees F for 35 minutes.
2. Divide into bowls and serve right away.

Basil Beef

Prep time: 10 minutes

Cook time: 35 minutes

Servings: 4

INGREDIENTS

- 2 pounds beef stew meat, cubed
- 1 cup tomato sauce
- 1 cup cherry tomatoes, halved
- 2 tablespoons basil, chopped
- 2 carrots, sliced
- 2 garlic cloves, minced
- Salt and black pepper to the taste

INSTRUCTIONS

1. In a pan that fits your air fryer, mix the beef with the tomato sauce and the other ingredients, introduce the pan in the fryer and cook at 390 degrees F for 35 minutes.
2. Divide the mix between plates and serve.

Lamb and Cauliflower Mix

Prep time: 10 minutes

Cook time: 25 minutes

Servings: 4

INGREDIENTS

- 2 pounds lamb chops
- 1 cup cauliflower florets
- 2 tablespoons butter, melted
- 1 teaspoon sweet paprika
- 2 tablespoons balsamic vinegar
- 1 garlic clove, minced
- A pinch of salt and black pepper
- ½ cup beef stock

INSTRUCTIONS

1. In a pan that fits your air fryer, mix the lamb chops with the cauliflower and the other ingredients, toss, introduce in the fryer and cook at 390 degrees F for 25 minutes.
2. Divide into bowls and serve.

AMATRICIANA

Prep time: 0-10 minutes

Cook time: 15-30 minutes

Servings: 4

INGREDIENTS

- 200g Pork cheek
- 1 Medium onion
- 400g Peeled tomatoes
- 3 spoons Oil
- 1 Chile
- Salt

INSTRUCTIONS

1. Chop the onion and cut the pork cheek (removing the hard shell). Put everything in the basket, adding the oil.
2. Close the cover, set the air fryer to 3 minutes at 150oC to brown. Then pour the tomato, pepper, and salt.
3. Cook for an additional 17 minutes, or until desired cooking is achieved.

Sweet Veggies Roasted Pork Chops

Prep time: 20 minutes

Cook time: 30 minutes

Servings: 6

INGREDIENTS

- 2 pounds Pork Chops, bone-in
- ½ tsp salt
- ½ tsp ground black pepper
- 3 carrots, chopped
- 2 celery stalks, chopped
- 1 Tbsp minced garlic
- 3 Tbsp butter, melted
- 2 Tbsp erythritol sweetener
- ½ cup white onion, chopped
- 1 tsp dried thyme
- ½ tsp dried rosemary

INSTRUCTIONS

1. Preheat your air fryer to 425 degrees F and prepare your air fryer tray with a piece of foil.
2. Rub the pork chops with the salt and pepper, wrap and let sit overnight to season.
3. Place the onion, carrot, celery and garlic on the prepared foil lined tray. Sprinkle the erythritol over the veggies.
4. Place the pork chops on top of the veggies.
5. Brush the pork chops with the melted butter and sprinkle with the thyme and rosemary.
6. Bake in the air fryer for 30 minutes or until the chicken thighs are browned and the veggies are beginning to brown as well.
7. Serve hot.

Zucchini Bacon Rollups

Prep time: 5 minutes

Cook time: 8 minutes

Servings: 8

INGREDIENTS

- 1 eggplant, sliced thinly lengthwise
- 4 oz mozzarella cheese, sliced
- 8 strips bacon
- 2 Tbsp chopped fresh basil
- 2 Tbsp olive oil

INSTRUCTIONS

1. Preheat your air fryer to 400 degrees F and prepare a large baking dish with foil.
2. Lay the eggplant slices out on a clean work surface.
3. Place a piece of cheese and a little basil on each eggplant slice and then roll up to enclose the filling.
4. Wrap a strip of bacon around the outside of each rollup.
5. Secure using a toothpick and then place the eggplant rolls on the prepared foil lined baking dish.
6. Drizzle with the olive oil and place in the air fryer to cook for 8 minutes. The eggplant should be lightly brown and the cheese melted. Serve warm.

Extra Juicy Meatballs

Prep time: 10 minutes

Cook time: 25 minutes

Servings: 4

INGREDIENTS

- 1 pound ground beef
- ¾ cup mozzarella cheese, shredded
- ¼ cup mayonnaise
- 1 egg
- ¼ cup fresh grated parmesan
- 1 tsp Italian seasoning
- ¼ tsp ground black pepper
- ¼ tsp salt
- 1 Tbsp almond flour

INSTRUCTIONS

1. Preheat your air fryer to 350 degrees F and line the air fryer tray with a piece of foil.
2. In a large mixing bowl, combine the beef, cheeses, mayonnaise, egg, Italian seasoning, pepper, salt and almond flour. Blend together well.
3. Roll the meat mixture into evenly sized balls and place on the prepared tray.
4. Bake for 25 minutes.
5. Serve the meatballs while hot!

Cauliflower and Bacon Fritters

Prep time: 10 minutes

Cook time: 30 minutes

Servings: 4

INGREDIENTS

- ¾ cup almond flour
- 7 Tbsp ground flaxseeds
- 1 cup cauliflower, fresh
- ½ cup cooked, crumbled bacon
- 4 ounces grated mozzarella cheese
- 2 eggs
- 2 tsp baking powder
- 1 tsp salt
- ¼ tsp ground black pepper
- 1 Tbsp olive oil

INSTRUCTIONS

1. Preheat your air fryer to 400 degrees F and prepare a large baking dish with foil.
2. Place the cauliflower in a food processor along with the mozzarella, bacon, almond flour, 4 tablespoons of the flaxseeds and baking powder. Pulse until the mixture reaches a crumbly texture.
3. Add the eggs, salt and pepper and pulse until a dough forms.
4. Scoop the mix into bite sized balls, rolling them between your hands.
5. Roll the balls in the remaining flaxseeds and place on the prepared baking tray.
6. Drizzle with the olive oil and roll the balls around on the tray so the olive oil is coating the outside.
7. Place in the preheated air fryer and bake for 10 minutes or until nicely golden brown. Enjoy hot.

Spicy Meatballs

Prep time: 10 minutes

Cook time: 25 minutes

Servings: 4

INGREDIENTS

- 1 pound ground beef
- ¾ cup mozzarella cheese, shredded
- ¼ cup fresh grated parmesan
- 1 tsp Italian seasoning
- 1 tsp cayenne pepper
- ¼ tsp ground black pepper
- ¼ tsp salt
- 1 Tbsp almond flour

INSTRUCTIONS

1. Preheat your air fryer to 350 degrees F and line the air fryer tray with a piece of foil.
2. In a large mixing bowl, combine the beef, cayenne pepper, cheeses, Italian seasoning, pepper, salt and almond flour. Blend together well.
3. Roll the meat mixture into evenly sized balls and place on the prepared tray.
4. Bake for 25 minutes.
5. Serve the meatballs while hot!

BEEF WITH LENTILS AND KIDNEY BEANS

Prep time: 10 minutes

Cook time: 35 minutes

Servings: 4

INGREDIENTS

- 1 pound beef stew meat, cubed
- 1 cup canned lentils, drained and rinsed
- 1 cup canned kidney beans, drained and rinsed
- 1 yellow onion, chopped
- 2 tablespoons olive oil
- Salt and black pepper to the taste
- 2 garlic cloves, minced
- 1 cup tomato sauce

INSTRUCTIONS

1. In the air fryer's pan, mix the beef with the lentils and the other ingredients, toss, transfer the pan to your air fryer and cook at 380 degrees F for 35 minutes.
2. Divide everything into bowls and serve.

Chili Ground Beef Mix

Prep time: 10 minutes

Cook time: 25 minutes

Servings: 4

INGREDIENTS

- 2 tablespoons butter, melted
- 1 pound beef meat, ground and browned
- 1 red onion, chopped
- 2 red chilies, minced
- 1 teaspoon chili powder
- 1 cup tomato sauce
- Salt and black pepper to the taste
- 2 garlic cloves, minced
- ½ teaspoon rosemary, dried
- 1 tablespoon parsley, chopped

INSTRUCTIONS

1. In the air fryer's pan, mix the melted butter with the browned beef and the other ingredients, introduce the pan in the fryer and cook at 380 degrees F for 14 minutes more.
2. Divide everything into bowls and serve.

FRIED PORK

Prep time: 10 – 20 minutes

Cook time: 0 – 15 minutes

Servings: 4

INGREDIENTS
- 300 g pork loin
- 2 egg yolks
- 4 tsp Worcestershire sauce:
- Salt to taste
- Taste Flour
- Gusto breadcrumbs

INSTRUCTIONS
1. Put the egg yolk, Worcestershire sauce and some flour (to thicken the sauce) in a bowl.
2. Cut the meat into pieces, lightly salt, and then pass it first in the sauce (previously prepared) and in breadcrumbs.
3. Grease the basket of the air fryer.
4. Preheat the air fryer for 1 minute at 200oC.
5. Add the pork and cook for 10 minutes, turning the meat halfway through cooking.

Perfect Garlic Butter Steak

Preparation: 20 min. –
Cook time: 12 min.

INGREDIENTS
- 2 Ribeye steaks
- Salt
- Pepper
- Olive oil
- Garlic butter:
- ½ cup softened butter
- 2 tbsp chopped fresh parsley
- 2 garlic cloves, minced
- 1 tsp Worcestershire sauce
- ½ tsp salt (optional)

INSTRUCTIONS :
- Prepare the garlic butter by mixing all the ingredients together.
- Place in parchment paper. Roll up and put in the fridge.
- Let the steaks sit for 20 minutes at room temperature.
- Brush with a little oil, salt, and pepper.
- Preheat your hot air fryer to 400°F (200°C).
- Cook for 12 minutes, turning halfway through cooking. Serve.
- Place the garlic butter on the steaks and let sit for 5 minutes.
- Enjoy!

Dijon Roasted Pork Chops

Prep time: 20 minutes

Cook time: 30 minutes

Servings: 6

INGREDIENTS

- 2 pounds Pork Chops, bone-in
- ½ tsp salt
- ½ tsp ground black pepper
- ¼ cup Dijon mustard
- 3 carrots, chopped
- 2 celery stalks, chopped
- 1 Tbsp minced garlic
- 3 Tbsp butter, melted
- ½ cup white onion, chopped
- 1 tsp dried thyme
- ½ tsp dried rosemary

INSTRUCTIONS

1. Preheat your air fryer to 425 degrees F and prepare your air fryer tray with a piece of foil.
2. Rub the pork chops with the salt, pepper, and Dijon and wrap and let sit overnight to season.
3. Place the onion, carrot, celery and garlic on the prepared foil lined tray.
4. Place the pork chops on top of the veggies.
5. Brush the pork chops with the melted butter and sprinkle with the thyme and rosemary.
6. Bake in the air fryer for 30 minutes or until the chicken thighs are browned and the veggies are beginning to brown as well.
7. Serve hot.

Lamb and Peppers Mix

Prep time: 10 minutes

Cook time: 25 minutes

Servings: 4

INGREDIENTS

- 2 pounds lamb chops
- 2 tablespoons butter, melted
- 1 red bell pepper, cut into strips
- 1 green bell pepper, cut into strips
- 1 yellow bell pepper, cut in strips
- 1 cup tomato sauce
- Salt and black pepper to the taste
- 1 tablespoon dill, chopped

INSTRUCTIONS

1. In a pan that fits your air fryer, mix the lamb chops with the melted butter and the other ingredients, toss, introduce the pan in the fryer and cook at 390 degrees F for 25 minutes.
2. Divide the mix between plates and serve.

Coriander Pork Steaks

Prep time: 10 minutes

Cook time: 20 minutes

Servings: 4

INGREDIENTS

- 1 tablespoon coriander, chopped
- 2 tablespoons avocado oil
- 4 pork steaks
- 1 teaspoon chili powder
- Salt and black pepper to the taste
- 1 tablespoon chives, chopped
- Juice of 1 lime

INSTRUCTIONS

1. In your air fryer's basket, mix the pork steaks with the coriander and the other ingredients, rub and cook at 390 degrees F for 10 minutes on each side.
2. Divide the steaks between plates and serve with a side salad.

Eggplant Bacon Caprese Rollups

Prep time: 5 minutes

Cook time: 8 minutes

Servings: 8

INGREDIENTS

- 1 eggplant, sliced thinly lengthwise
- 4 oz mozzarella cheese, sliced
- 8 strips bacon
- 1 tomato, sliced
- 2 Tbsp chopped fresh basil
- 2 Tbsp olive oil

INSTRUCTIONS

1. Preheat your air fryer to 400 degrees F and prepare a large baking dish with foil.
2. Lay the eggplant slices out on a clean work surface.
3. Place a piece of tomato, cheese and a little basil on each eggplant slice and then roll up to enclose the filling.
4. Wrap a strip of bacon around the outside of each rollup.
5. Secure using a toothpick and then place the eggplant rolls on the prepared foil lined baking dish.
6. Drizzle with the olive oil and place in the air fryer to cook for 8 minutes. The eggplant should be lightly brown and the cheese melted. Serve warm.

Veggies Roasted Pork Chops

Prep time: 20 minutes

Cook time: 30 minutes

Servings: 6

INGREDIENTS

- 2 pounds Pork Chops, bone-in
- ½ tsp salt
- ½ tsp ground black pepper
- 3 carrots, chopped
- 2 celery stalks, chopped
- 1 Tbsp minced garlic
- 3 Tbsp butter, melted
- ½ cup white onion, chopped
- 1 tsp dried thyme
- ½ tsp dried rosemary

INSTRUCTIONS

1. Preheat your air fryer to 425 degrees F and prepare your air fryer tray with a piece of foil.
2. Rub the pork chops with the salt and pepper, wrap and let sit overnight to season.
3. Place the onion, carrot, celery and garlic on the prepared foil lined tray.
4. Place the pork chops on top of the veggies.
5. Brush the pork chops with the melted butter and sprinkle with the thyme and rosemary.
6. Bake in the air fryer for 30 minutes or until the chicken thighs are browned and the veggies are beginning to brown as well.
7. Serve hot.

BACON AND CHEESE CASSEROLE

Prep time: 10 minutes

Cook time: 30 minutes

Servings: 12

INGREDIENTS

- 16 eggs
- ¼ cup whole milk
- 1 cup cooked, sliced bacon
- 1 cup cheddar cheese, grated
- ½ cup grated parmesan cheese
- ½ cup whole milk ricotta
- ¼ cup chopped white onion
- 1 tsp minced garlic
- 1 tsp sea salt
- ½ tsp dried thyme
- ½ tsp ground black pepper

INSTRUCTIONS

1. Preheat your air fryer to 350 degrees F and prepare a large baking dish with baking grease (make sure the pan will fit in your air fryer.
2. Whisk the eggs and milk in a large bowl.
3. Add the bacon to the egg mix.
4. Add all the remaining ingredients, except the ricotta, and stir well.
5. Pour the egg and veggie mix into the prepared tray.
6. Dollop the ricotta around the pan, dispersing it evenly.
7. Bake in the air fryer for 30 minutes or until the eggs are completely set.

Lamb Meatballs

Prep time: 10 minutes

Cook time: 25 minutes

Servings: 4

INGREDIENTS

- 1 pound ground lamb
- ¾ cup mozzarella cheese, shredded
- ¼ cup fresh grated parmesan
- 1 tsp Italian seasoning
- ¼ tsp ground black pepper
- ¼ tsp salt
- 1 Tbsp almond flour

INSTRUCTIONS

1. Preheat your air fryer to 350 degrees F and line the air fryer tray with a piece of foil.
2. In a large mixing bowl, combine the lamb, cheeses, Italian seasoning, pepper, salt and almond flour. Blend together well.
3. Roll the meat mixture into evenly sized balls and place on the prepared tray.
4. Bake for 25 minutes.
5. Serve the meatballs while hot!

Beef, Corn and Sweet Potatoes

Prep time: 10 minutes

Cook time: 35 minutes

Servings: 4

INGREDIENTS

- 2 pounds beef stew meat, cubed
- 2 sweet potatoes, peeled and cubed
- 1 tablespoon olive oil
- 1 cup corn
- 1 tablespoon rosemary, chopped
- 1 cup tomato sauce
- Juice of 1 lemon
- 2 garlic cloves, minced
- Salt and black pepper to the taste

INSTRUCTIONS

1. In the air fryer's pan, mix the beef with the potatoes and the other ingredients, toss well, introduce the pan in the fryer and cook at 390 degrees F for 35 minutes.
2. Divide between plates and serve..

Sautéed Meat with Potatoes

Prep time: 10-20 minutes

Cook time: 30-45 minutes

Servings: 6

INGREDIENTS

- 750g beef
- 350 g of potatoes
- 200 ml of hot broth
- 250 g of tomato coulis
- 1 onion
- Salt to taste
- Pepper to taste

INSTRUCTIONS :

1. Chop the onion and put it in the basket previously greased.
2. Set the temperature to 150OC.
3. Brown the onion for 3 to 4 minutes and then add the pieces of meat, broth, salt, and pepper.
4. Cook the meat for 20 minutes and add the potatoes and the tomato coulis.
5. Cook for another 20 to 25 minutes, mixing the sautéed with a wooden spoon 3 to 4 times during cooking to prevent it from drying out too much.

Lamb with Potatoes

Prep time: 10-20 minutes

Cook time: 30 - 45 minutes

Servings: 2

INGREDIENTS

- 1 kg Lamb milk in pieces
- 600g Fresh potatoes
- 5 spoons Sunflower oil
- Salt and pepper
- 2 spoons Sage, rosemary, thyme
- ½ glass White wine

INSTRUCTIONS

1. Remove the mixing paddle from the tank.
2. Put the pieces of lamb, oil, sage, rosemary, and thyme in the cooking pot. Close the cover, set the thermostat to position 4, press the lower resistance power key and press the on / off key; brown for 4 min.
3. Add the wine and simmer for another 6 min.
4. Preheat the air fryer at 1500C for 5 minutes.
5. Finally pour the potatoes cut into pieces, salt, pepper and cook for 35 min. Extra by mixing the potatoes manually 2-3 times during cooking.

GARLIC AND LIME BEEF

Prep time: 10 minutes

Cook time: 30 minutes

Servings: 4

INGREDIENTS

- 2 tablespoons olive oil
- 2 pounds beef stew meat, cubed
- 3 garlic cloves, minced
- Juice of 1 lime
- 1 tablespoon sweet paprika
- Salt and black pepper to the taste
- 1 tablespoon rosemary, chopped

INSTRUCTIONS

1. In the air fryer's pan, mix the beef with the garlic and the other ingredients, toss and cook at 390 degrees F for 30 minutes.
2. Divide between plates and serve.

VEAL BLANQUETTE WITH PEAS

Prep time: 10-20

Cook time: 45-60

Servings: 2

INGREDIENTS

- 600g Veal meat
- 250g Frozen peas
- ½ Onions
- ½ glass White wine
- 1 tsp Oil
- 250 ml Broth

INSTRUCTIONS

1. Chop the onion and put it inside the tank with the oil. Close the lid
2. Brown for 5 min setting the air fryer at 150OC.
3. Add lightly floured meat, white wine, and simmer for 10 minutes.
4. Then add frozen peas, broth, salt, pepper, and simmer for 35 minutes. additional depending on the desired degree of cooking.

Broccoli and Bacon Fritters

Prep time: 10 minutes

Cook time: 30 minutes

Servings: 4

INGREDIENTS

- ¾ cup almond flour
- 7 Tbsp ground flaxseeds
- 1 cup broccoli, fresh
- ½ cup cooked, crumbled bacon
- 4 ounces grated mozzarella cheese
- 2 eggs
- 2 tsp baking powder
- 1 tsp salt
- ¼ tsp ground black pepper
- 1 Tbsp olive oil

INSTRUCTIONS

1. Preheat your air fryer to 400 degrees F and prepare a large baking dish with foil.
2. Place the broccoli in a food processor along with the mozzarella, bacon, almond flour, 4 tablespoons of the flaxseeds and baking powder. Pulse until the mixture reaches a crumbly texture.
3. Add the eggs, salt and pepper and pulse until a dough forms.
4. Scoop the mix into bite sized balls, rolling them between your hands.
5. Roll the balls in the remaining flaxseeds and place on the prepared baking tray.
6. Drizzle with the olive oil and roll the balls around on the tray so the olive oil is coating the outside.
7. Place in the preheated air fryer and bake for 10 minutes or until nicely golden brown. Enjoy hot.

Meatballs with Tomatoes and Peas

Prep time: 10 – 20

Cook time: 15 - 30, 6 people.

INGREDIENTS

- 425 g minced meat
- 1 egg
- 25 g grated cheese
- Salt to taste
- To taste breadcrumbs
- Parsley chopped to taste
- 150 g of frozen peas
- 400 g of tomatoes cut into large pieces
- 1 tsp oil
- 2 shallots

INSTRUCTIONS

1. Put the minced meat, the egg, the grated cheese, the salt, the parsley, the breadcrumbs in a bowl and mix until you get a consistent mixture. Form the meatballs (with these doses you will get 15-18 meatballs).
2. Chop the shallots and pour them into the basket greased with the oil. Close. Set the air fryer at 150OC and brown for 3 min.
3. Add the meatballs and simmer for an additional 7 minutes.
4. Then add the frozen peas, tomato, salt and pepper and simmer for another 18 minutes.

Beef Stroganoff

Prep time: 10-20

Cook time: 15 – 30

Servings: 6

INGREDIENTS

- 1000 g beef
- 500g onion
- Mushrooms 500g
- 150g sour cream
- 50 g butter
- 100 g of broth
- Salt, pepper to taste
- 2 tbsp paprika
- Flour

INSTRUCTIONS

1. Cut the onion into very thin slices, then clean the mushrooms well and cut them into slices, finally cut the meat into strips about 5 cm long.
2. Place the butter, onion, and mushrooms on the baking sheet.
3. Preheat the air fryer at 200C for 5 minutes. Simmer for 10 min.
4. Add the floured meat, paprika, broth, salt, pepper, and simmer for another 10 minutes.
5. Finally pour the cream and finish cooking for another 5 minutes or until ready.

Baharat Lamb Meatballs

Prep time: 10 minutes

Cook time: 25 minutes

Servings: 4

INGREDIENTS

- 1 pound ground lamb
- ¾ cup halloumi cheese, shredded
- ¼ cup fresh grated parmesan
- 1 tsp Baharat seasoning
- ¼ tsp ground black pepper
- ¼ tsp salt
- 1 Tbsp coconut flour

INSTRUCTIONS

1. Preheat your air fryer to 350 degrees F and line the air fryer tray with a piece of foil.
2. In a large mixing bowl, combine the lamb, cheeses, Baharat seasoning, pepper, salt and coconut flour. Blend together well.
3. Roll the meat mixture into evenly sized balls and place on the prepared tray.
4. Bake for 25 minutes.
5. Serve the meatballs while hot!

Lamb and Shallots Mix

Prep time: 10 minutes

Cook time: 35 minutes

Servings: 4

INGREDIENTS

- 2 pounds lamb stew meat, cubed
- 1 cup shallots, chopped
- 1 cup red wine
- 1 tablespoon rosemary, chopped
- 1 teaspoon chili powder
- 2 garlic cloves, minced
- 2 tablespoons chives, chopped
- Salt and black pepper to the taste

INSTRUCTIONS

1. In the air fryer's pan, mix the lamb with the shallots and the other ingredients, transfer the pan to your air fryer and cook at 380 degrees F for 35 minutes.
2. Divide everything into bowls and serve.

Printed in Great Britain
by Amazon

16214659R00050